Surprising Ways Animals Snooze

SLEEPY

All animals sleep.
But not all animals sleep in
the same way. Because when
you are sleepy, if you're a . . .

written by Jennifer Ward illustrated by Robin Page

Beach Lane Books New York London Toronto Sydney New Delhi

dolphin,

maybe you will join your pod?
Side by side you'll swim and nod.
Or become a floating log,
resting in a dreamy fog.

A dolphin is a mammal that must swim to
the water's surface to breathe air through
its blowhole into its lungs. But how can a
dolphin both swim and sleep? By sleeping
with one half of its brain awake while the
other rests! During this half-sleeping-brain
stage, called "unihemispheric slow-wave
sleep," a dolphin can both rest and swim
near the water's surface. Or a dolphin might
sleep by floating on the water's surface, a
behavior called "logging."

If you're a . . .

little brown bat,

for twenty hours each day, you choose
to dangle upside down and snooze
in a cave or under bark
until the sky above is dark.

Little brown bats sleep longer than most
mammals, averaging about twenty hours per
day. Their resting place is called a "roost."
During spring and summer, females may
roost together with their pups in natural
spaces, such as tree cavities, or man-made
spaces, such as attics. Males usually roost
alone under tree bark or in tree cavities,
woodpiles, or rock piles. Little brown bats
wake up in the evening to hunt for insects
to eat. During winter, little brown bats move
into hibernacula, such as caves or mines,
where they hibernate in large colonies.

If you're a . . .

hummingbird,

torpor is your type of sleep—
it's a sleep that's *very* deep!
With toes around a branch quite tight,
you get your shut-eye through the night.

Everything works zippy-fast on a
hummingbird—its breathing, its heartbeat,
its wings. It eats tiny bugs and nectar all day
long to keep its needy and speedy body
alive. At night, it sleeps by gripping tightly
to a tiny branch with its toes and entering a
hibernation-like state called "torpor." During
torpor, its heart rate and breathing slow, and
its body temperature drops. It can take up
to an hour for a hummingbird to come out of
torpor each morning.

If you're a . . .

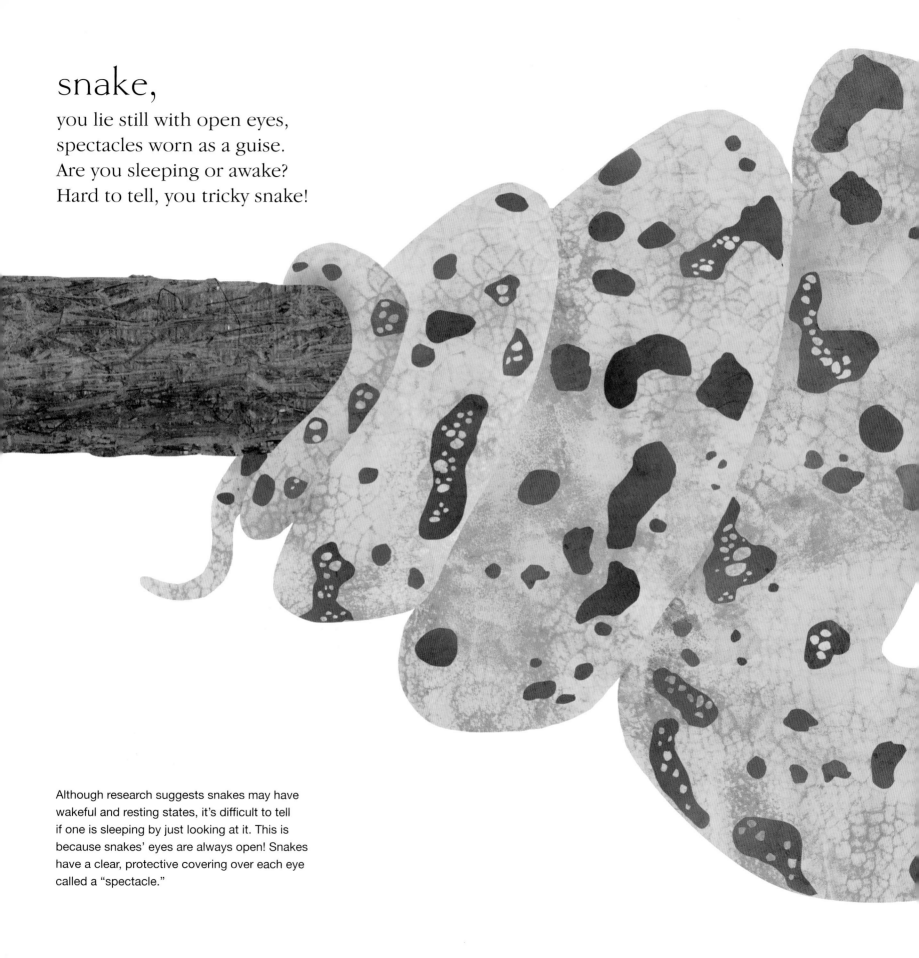

snake,

you lie still with open eyes,
spectacles worn as a guise.
Are you sleeping or awake?
Hard to tell, you tricky snake!

Although research suggests snakes may have
wakeful and resting states, it's difficult to tell
if one is sleeping by just looking at it. This is
because snakes' eyes are always open! Snakes
have a clear, protective covering over each eye
called a "spectacle."

If you're a . . .

sea otter,

in a raft you're holding hands—
also wrapped in seaweed bands—
so that you won't float away.
Side by side, you rest and stay.

Sea otters may hold hands with other otters
while resting. How cute is that? They do
this to remain with their raft, or group. In
addition, sea otters may wrap themselves in
kelp that is anchored to the ocean floor. This
prevents them from floating out to sea while
sleeping, grooming, and eating.

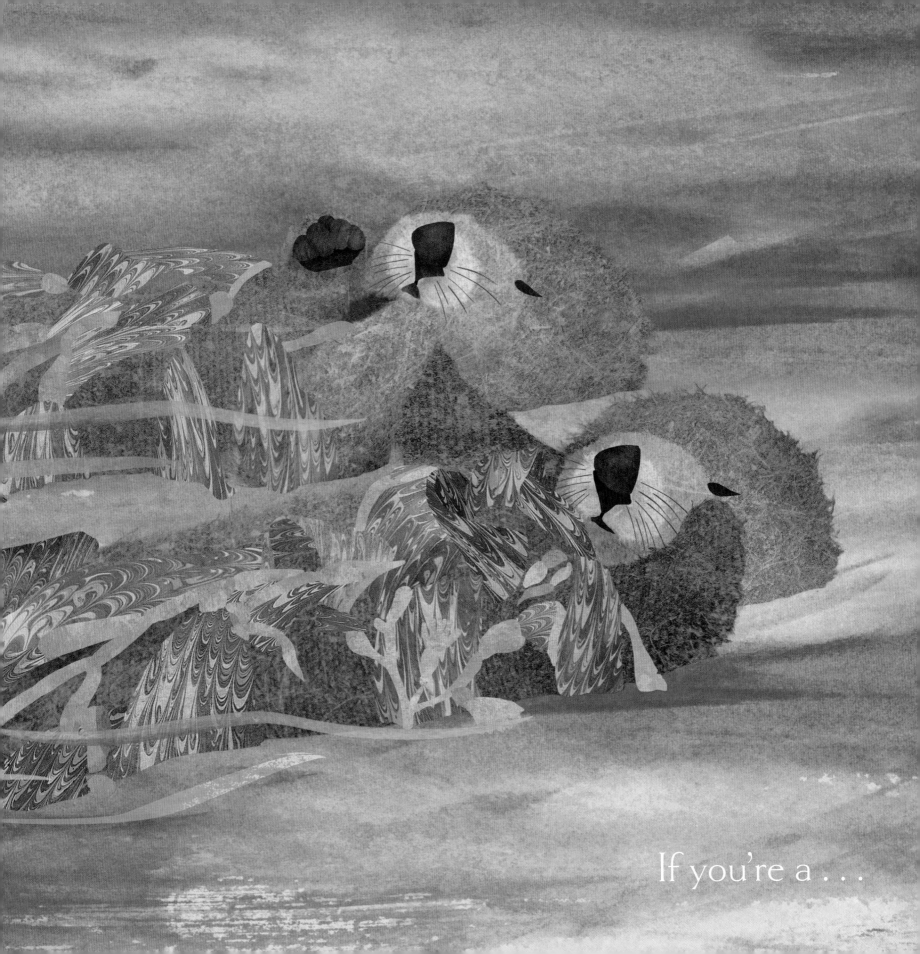

If you're a . . .

grizzly bear,

you slumber, snore, and lie quite still
through days and nights of winter's chill.
Once it's warm, you nap and forage,
building up your winter storage.

During winter, grizzly bears hibernate based on temperatures and food supplies. During hibernation, they do not eat, drink, or go to the bathroom. They live off a layer of fat built up during the summer and fall. When not hibernating, grizzly bears are busy finding food and sleep about nine hours each day.

If you're a . . .

humpback whale,

you fall into a slow-wave rest
as tides around you rise and crest.
Half awake and half asleep,
you doze within the ocean deep.

The humpback whale, like all whales, must
swim to the water's surface to breathe air
through its blowhole into its lungs. Similar to
dolphins, they sleep with one eye open, one
eye shut, and half their brain at rest while
the other half is alert (unihemispheric slow-
wave sleep). Scientists are working to learn
more about sleep in cetaceans (whales and
dolphins) and have documented humpback
whales resting not far from the ocean's
surface for blocks of time.

If you're a . . .

koala,

you are such a sleepyhead
in your eucalyptus bed.
You'll snack and chew an hour or two,
then back to sleep when you are through!

The koala wins the award for being the
sleepiest animal in the animal kingdom. It
eats only eucalyptus leaves, which do not
provide much nutrition and require a lot of
time to digest, so a koala sleeps around
twenty-two hours per day.

If you're a . . .

frog,

you hide beneath a log or leaf,
hushed and tucked. Your bedtime, brief.
In wintertime, you snuggle deep
and slowly, slowly, slowly sleep.

Most terrestrial frogs are active at night.
By day, they'll tuck into a spot that's moist
and safe. In winter, frogs enter a state of
brumation, a type of hibernation for cold-
blooded animals. During brumation, frogs'
activity, heart rate, and breathing slow, and
their body temperature drops.

If you're a . . .

giraffe,

when it's time to stop and doze,
you perform the perfect pose:
you curl your neck and place your head
upon your back—a giraffe bed!

Giraffes can sleep standing up or lying
down, but only for about five minutes at a
time—a pattern of sleep called "polyphasic
sleep."

If you're an . . .

African elephant,

you may lie down, but often stand
to slumber in your wild land.
Your trunk stops moving, keeping still—
a brief but mighty elephant chill.

Scientists believe elephants sleep less than
any other mammal in the wild, averaging
about two hours per day. Like giraffes, they
have polyphasic sleep and may even find a
tree to lean upon as they snooze.

If you're a . . .

sloth,

when you're not snacking, you are sleeping.
That's the type of day you're keeping!
Then—*Yawn!*—you curl into a ball,
snug in a tree so you won't fall.

Sloths spend most of their time in trees, and
some even spend their entire lives in the
same tree where they were born! Sleeping
up to ten hours per day, a sloth may curl into
a tree's fork or sleep while hanging by its
claws from branches.

If you're a . . .

desert tortoise,

when summer days are dry and hot,
you dig yourself a cooler spot
deep in the ground for a time-out,
until it cools or there's no drought.

Temperatures in the Mojave and Sonoran Deserts during the summer can exceed 104 degrees Fahrenheit (41 degrees Celsius). To escape the extreme heat, a desert tortoise will dig a burrow to wait out the weather for days or even weeks at a time. There, it becomes inactive, not leaving to find food, eat, or go to the bathroom—a type of rest that conserves energy, called "estivation."

If you're a . . .

nurse shark,

you snuggle on the ocean floor
in a group with many more,
then rest on sand so soft and white,
until the day becomes the night.

Nurse sharks spend the daytime resting
together at the ocean's bottom. They can
remain still in water, unlike great white sharks,
which must constantly move through the
ocean to breathe. Nurse sharks are nocturnal,
waking at night to hunt alone.

If you're a . . .

great frigatebird,

you find a cloud and hitch a ride
on thermal drafts that help you glide
and circle upward, upward high
to catch a rest while on the fly.

Great frigatebirds fly over the ocean for up
to two months at a time without touching
down on land or water to rest. Unlike most
seabirds, frigatebirds can't swim! They use
unihemispheric slow-wave sleep (half-
sleeping brain) in short bursts while gliding
upward on the thermals (warm air currents)
formed beneath giant cumulus clouds.

If you're an . . .

orangutan,

each night you use a cozy nest,
high in treetops, where you rest,
weaving branches, leaves, and twigs
as bedding for the perfect digs.

All great apes, including orangutans, build beds for sleeping and napping. Orangutans use branches as bases and leaves for pillows, and make their beds high in the treetops where they live. There, they curl up and sleep soundly for eight to ten hours each night, just like people do.

If you're a . . .

child,

at sunrise you are on the go!
But once it's dark, it's time to slow
and snuggle, sleeping through the night,
while waiting for the morning light.

Sleep for children (and adults) takes place during one long period of time, usually at night. This is called "monophasic sleep."

Hey, sleepyhead, don't nod off yet!
There's more cool stuff to read below. . . .

Sleep patterns vary widely among animals. Animal sleep is based on many things, such as food supply, habitat, weather, and defense mechanisms. The one constant? *All* animals require sleep.

desert tortoise: 12 hours

grizzly bear (not hibernating): 8–10 hours

Types of Sleep in This Book

brumation: a hibernation-like state for cold-blooded animals that takes place when the weather is too cold for survival. A reptile or an amphibian, such as a frog, will find a safe place to rest until the weather is warmer. During brumation, the heart rate, breathing rate, and metabolic rate (how food is turned into energy) slow down so the animal may conserve energy.

estivation: a hibernation-like state for cold-blooded animals that takes place when the weather is too hot and dry for survival. An amphibian or a reptile, such as a tortoise, will burrow or find a shady, safe place to rest until the weather is less harsh. During estivation, the heart rate, breathing rate, and metabolic rate slow down so the animal may conserve energy.

hibernation: a prolonged state of rest for certain warm-blooded animals, such as bears, that takes place during winter. During hibernation, bears slow down their heart rate and breathing rate, and will not eat or go to the bathroom, to conserve energy and survive.

monophasic sleep: when an animal, such as people and other primates, sleeps in one block of time per day. This type of sleep usually takes place at night.

polyphasic sleep: when an animal sleeps several or many times a day for short periods of time. Most wild animals sleep this way, such as giraffes and elephants.

torpor: a type of sleep used by some animals, such as hummingbirds. During torpor, an animal's body temperature drops, and its heart rate, breathing, and metabolism slow.

unihemispheric slow-wave sleep: a sleep behavior where one half of the brain is awake while the other half is asleep.

Other Words to Wonder About

crepuscular: an animal that is most active during twilight

diurnal: an animal that sleeps at night and is awake during the day

nocturnal: an animal that is awake at night and sleeps during the day

Average Snooze Time for Animals in the Wild Per Day

dolphin: 8 hours

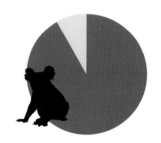

hummingbird: 12 hours

frog: 12 hours

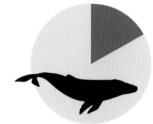

humpback whale: 4 hours

giraffe: 5 hours

koala: 22 hours

■ hours asleep

□ hours awake

■ unknown

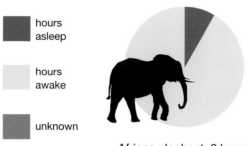

African elephant: 2 hours

great frigatebird (at sea): 45 minutes

little brown bat: 20 hours

nurse shark: 12 hours

infant: 14–17 hours

Average Snooze Time for People Per Day

orangutan: 8–10 hours

toddler: 11–14 hours

sea otter: 11 hours

preschool: 10–13 hours

sloth: 15 hours

school age: 9–12 hours

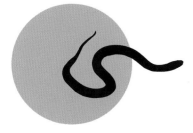

snake: unknown

adult: 7–9 hours

Selected Sources

Websites

Bat Conservation International: batcon.org
Florida Museum of Natural History: floridamuseum.ufl.edu
The National Wildlife Federation: nwf.org
Oceana: oceana.org

Articles

Glendinning, David R., Alexandra J. Reddy, Elizabeth S. Herrelko, Melba Brown, Elizabeth Renner, and Laurie Thompson. "The Nuances of Orangutan Nests." Smithsonian's National Zoo & Conservation Biology Institute, (August 30, 2018). https://nationalzoo.si.edu/animals/news/nuances-orangutan-nests.

Hicks, James W., and Marvin L. Riedesel. "Diurnal Ventilatory Patterns in the Garter Snake, *Thamnophis elegans*." Journal of Comparative Physiology, 149, (December 1983): 503–10. https://link.springer.com/article/10.1007/BF00690009.

Langley, Liz. "These Birds Nap While They Fly—and Other Surprising Ways That Animals Sleep." National Geographic, (May 3, 2021). https://www.nationalgeographic.com/animals/article/surprising-ways-that-animals-sleep.

Meinch, Tree. "Animals That Sleep the Least and the Most." Discover Magazine, (November 13, 2020). https://www.discovermagazine.com/planet-earth/animals-that-sleep-the-least-and-the-most.

VanHelder, Mike. "Scientists Finally Have Evidence That Frigatebirds Sleep While Flying." National Audubon Society, (August 11, 2016). www.audubon.org/news/scientists-finally-have-evidence-frigatebirds-sleep-while-flying.

White, Robyn. "How Do Sharks Sleep? With Both Eyes Open, Scientists Discover." Newsweek, (March 8, 2022). https://www.newsweek.com/how-do-sharks-sleep-both-eyes-open-1685993.

Acknowledgments

With gratitude to Dr. Charles Robbins, professor and director of research, WSU Bear Research, Education, and Conservation Center, and Dr. Heiko Jansen, professor, Integrative Physiology and Neuroscience, College of Veterinary Medicine at Washington State University and WSU Bear Research, Education, and Conservation Center. And a big mahalo to Marc O. Lammers, PhD, research ecologist, Hawaiian Islands Humpback Whale National Marine Sanctuary. Thank you all for sharing such interesting insights regarding your research and information about animal sleep.

BEACH LANE BOOKS

An imprint of Simon & Schuster Children's Publishing Division • 1230 Avenue of the Americas, New York, New York 10020 • Text © 2024 by Jennifer Ward • Illustration © 2024 by Robin Page • Book design by Irene Metaxatos • All rights reserved, including the right of reproduction in whole or in part in any form. • BEACH LANE BOOKS and colophon are trademarks of Simon & Schuster, LLC. • Simon & Schuster: Celebrating 100 Years of Publishing in 2024 • For information about special discounts for bulk purchases, please contact Simon & Schuster Special Sales at 1-866-506-1949 or business@simonandschuster.com. • The Simon & Schuster Speakers Bureau can bring authors to your live event. • For more information or to book an event, contact the Simon & Schuster Speakers Bureau at 1-866-248-3049 or visit our website at www.simonspeakers.com. • The text for this book was set in Goldenbook, ITC Garamond BT, and Helvetica Neue. • The illustrations for this book were rendered in Photoshop. • Manufactured in China • 0324 SCP • First Edition • 10 9 8 7 6 5 4 2 1 • Library of Congress Cataloging-in-Publication Data • Names: Ward, Jennifer, author. | Page, Robin, illustrator. • Title: Sleepy : surprising ways animals snooze / Jennifer Ward, illustrated by Robin Page. • Description: First edition. | New York : Beach Lane Books, 2024. | Includes bibliographical references. | Audience: Ages 4–8 | Audience: Grades 2–3 | Summary: "Across the animal kingdom, there are a whole lot of ways animals snooze. Different species have their own fascinating sleep patterns and habits"— Provided by publisher. • Identifiers: LCCN 2023032047 (print) | LCCN 2023032048 (ebook) | ISBN 9781665935104 (hardcover) | ISBN 9781665935111 (ebook) • Subjects: LCSH: Sleep behavior in animals—Juvenile literature. | Animal behavior—Juvenile literature. | Sleep—Juvenile literature. • Classification: LCC QL755.3.W37 2024 (print) | LCC QL755.3 (ebook) | DDC 591.5/19—dc23/eng/20230803 • LC record available at https://lccn.loc.gov/2023032047 • LC ebook record available at https://lccn.loc.gov/2023032048

For Di Doster (and crew!) at
Wild Bird Rehabilitation in St. Louis, Missouri,
a tireless group helping songbirds

—J. W.

For Ash

—R. P.